Why Documents Matter:
AMERICAN ORIGINALS AND
THE HISTORICAL IMAGINATION

Selections from the
Gilder Lehrman Collection

edited by James G. Basker

The Gilder Lehrman Institute of American History
New York City
2007

INTRODUCTION

This booklet of historic documents, presented in facsimile and transcription, has been compiled to provide materials for teachers at every level, k-12 and beyond. In many states and districts, teachers and their students are preparing to meet guidelines and take examinations that require close attention to single documents. The educational benefits from such an approach can be numerous: students learn to read closely, to interpret documents in historical context, to ground argument in concrete evidence, and to explicate larger historical meanings from primary sources. But perhaps above all, such documents can be a stimulus to the imagination. They can "humanize" history. And once the imagination is engaged, there is no limit to learning.

So, for example, students can compare the two versions of the U.S. Constitution included here, one a draft, the other the final version, and discover that the delegates who initially regarded themselves as representing "the States of New-Hampshire, Massachusetts, Rhode Island . . ." within a few weeks had reconceived themselves as "We, the People of the United States." What person, whether fourth-grader or high school senior, can witness the moment of such a transformation and not be moved? Another document in this collection touches on human weakness and tragedy: it is the letter written by Angelica Church on July 11, 1804 upon hearing that her brother-in-law (and by some accounts, her lover) Alexander Hamilton had been wounded in a duel by "that wretch Burr." Mistaken in her belief that Hamilton would recover (he died the following day), Angelica scrawls the letter in such haste that her handwriting betrays the depth of her emotional upset. A third example touches different emotions. It is the letter written in 1857 by Frederick Douglass, now a free man and a famous abolitionist in the North, to his former master Hugh Auld back in Maryland. Certainly one of the only letters ever written by a former slave to his master, it challenges us to fathom the depths of humanity and understanding in a man who could write: "I feel nothing but kindness for you all - I love you, but hate slavery."

These and some two dozen other documents printed here are all drawn from the Gilder Lehrman Collection, a collection of more than 60,000 important American historical documents, now on deposit at the New-York Historical Society in New York City. Richard Gilder and Lewis Lehrman, the philanthropists and history lovers who compiled the collection over many years, wanted it not to languish in a vault, but to reach the largest possible audience and to be useful especially for teachers and students. They founded the Gilder Lehrman Institute of American History in 1994 and charged it with doing everything possible "to promote the study and love of American history," particularly by disseminating and making available in various media the rare historic documents in their collection.

Teachers, students, or general readers who find the documents in this booklet useful may want to consult the Gilder Lehrman Institute website at www.gilderlehrman.org, where they will find primary materials and historic documents from the colonial era to the 20th century. They appear in many formats in different areas of the site: as facsimiles, and in virtual exhibitions, curriculum modules, newly discovered document features, and a comprehensive digital catalog which can be searched by author, subject, date, or accession number. And the whole of the site can be searched by name or keyword, enabling even the casual visitor to immediately search comprehensively for all documents concerning "George Washington" or "Frederick Douglass" or "the Civil War."

Visitors to the Gilder Lehrman website will also learn about the many other programs and publications the Institute has created for teachers, students, and the general public. Every summer GLI sponsors more than 20 one-week seminars that bring history teachers into residence with leading historians such as James McPherson, Eric Foner, Allen Guelzo, Drew Faust, Joyce Appleby, Ken Jackson, and many others. The Institute publishes history calendars, facsimile documents, interactive CD-ROMs, history journals, and other resources for the classroom. It underwrites traveling exhibitions on such topics as the history of abolition that tour the country and offers fellowships for teachers to attend scholarly conferences. It partners with local education authorities to develop history schools – schools in which students essentially "major" in history, taking a course in American history each semester for four years.

Please contact us directly if you are interested in bringing any of what we offer into your school or community. And meanwhile, I hope you enjoy these two dozen examples of "why documents matter."

JAMES G. BASKER
President, Gilder Lehrman Institute of American History
Richard Gilder Professor of Literary History, Barnard College, Columbia University

THE BOSTON MASSACRE, 1770: *This hand-colored engraving by Paul Revere, artisan and patriot, elevates a street skirmish in Boston in 1770 into a "Massacre." A brilliant piece of propaganda, it galvanized the colonists' sentiments against repressive policies of the British.* (Paul Revere, "The Bloody Massacre perpetrated in King-Street, Boston on March 5, 1770," 1770. From the Gilder Lehrman Collection, GLC 2290.)

THE DECLARATION OF INDEPENDENCE, 1776: *First printed in Philadelphia in July 1776, it was then sent to various cities and towns for reprinting and dissemination. This copy, which is the sole survivor of a Charleston, South Carolina, printing in August of 1776, did not surface until the 1990s. It is the first concrete proof that such a printing occurred, with the intention of spreading the news of American independence through the South Carolina hinterlands. By publishing his name the patriotic printer literally put his life on the line.*
(Declaration of Independence, printed by Peter Timothy in Charleston, S.C., ca. August 2, 1776. From the Gilder Lehrman Collection, GLC 959.)

LETTER FROM LUCY KNOX TO HER HUSBAND, GENERAL HENRY KNOX, 1777: Wife of Revolutionary War general Henry Knox and daughter of Loyalists who had fled to England at the start of the war, Lucy stayed in Boston when her husband joined the army. She writes of battlefield news, wartime profiteering, and family business, and suggests that when General Knox returns home he be open to "equal command."

I wish I had fifty guineas to spare to send by her for neccessarys– but I have not– the very little gold we have must be reserved for my Love in case he should be taken– for friends in such a case are not too common.

I am more distressed from the hott weather than any other fears– God grant you may not go farther southard– if you should I positively will come too– I believe Genl Howe is a paltry fellow.. but happy for as that he is so– are you not much pleased with the news from the Northard. We think it is a great affair and a confirmation of St. Clair's villainy baseness. I hope he will not go unpunished-we hear also that Genl Gates is to go back to his command if so Mister Schuyler cannot be guiltless– it is very strange, you never mentioned that affair in any of your letters-

What has become of Mrs. Green, do you all live together- or how do you manage- is Billy to remain with you payless or is he to have a commission- if the former I think he had much better remained where he was- if he understood business he might without a capital have made a fortune- people here-without advanceing a shilling frequently clear hundreds in a day- Such chaps as Eben Oliver, are all men of fortune- while persons who have ever lived in affluence, are in danger of want- oh that you had less of the military man about you- you might then after the war have lived at ease all the days of your life- but now I don't know what you will do- your *** being long acustomed to command- will make you too haughty for mercantile matters—tho I hope you will not consider yourself as commander in chief of your own house– but be convinced tho not in the affair of Mr. Coudoe that there is such a thing as equal command— I send this by Capt. Randal who says he expects to remain with you– pray how many of these lads have have you– I am sure they must be very expensive– I am in want of some square dollars– which I expect from you, to by me a peace of linen an article I can do no longer without haveing had no recruit of that kind for almost five years- girls in general when they marry- are well stocked with those things but poor I had no such advantage————**

little Lucy who is without exception the sweetest child in the world- sends you a

                    shall
kiss but where ^ I take it from say you- from the paper I hope- but dare I say I
                that
sometimes fear ~~what~~ a long absence the force of bad example may lead you to forget me at sometimes- to know that it even gave you pleasure to be in company with the finest woman in the world, would be worse than death to me- but it is not so, my Harry is too just too delicate too sincere- and too fond of his Lucy to admit the most remote thought of that distracting kind- away with it- don't be angry with me my love- I am not jealous of your affection- I love you with a love as true and sacred as ever entered the human heart- but from a diffidence of my own merit I sometimes fear you will love me less- after being so long from me- if you should may my life end before I know it- that I may die thinking you wholly mine- Adieu my love LK

* Throughout this publication, text written in a bold type indicates material shown in the image at right.

being long accustomed to command will make you too haughty for mercantile matters — tho I hope you will not consider yourself as commander in chief of your own house — but be convinced tho not in the affair of Mr Erskine that there is not a thing as equal command — I send this by Capt Randal who says he expects to remain with you — pray how many of these lads have have you — I am sure they must be very expensive — I am in want of some square dollars — which I expect from you — to by me a peace of linen an article — I can do no longer without haveing had no recruit of that kind for almost five years girls in general when they marry — are well stocked with those things but poor I had no such advantage ————————————

little Lucy who is without exception the sweetest child in the world — sends you a kiss — but where shall I take it from say you — know the propper I hope — but dare I say I sometimes fear that a long absence the force of bad example may lead you to forget me at some times — to know that it ever gave you pleasure to be in company with the finest woman in the world would be worse than death to me — but it is not so, my Harry is too just too delicate too sincere — and too kind to his Lucy to admit the most remote thought of that distracting kind — away with it ————

dont be angry with me my love — I am not jealous of your affection — I love you with a love as true and sacred as ever entered the human heart — but from a diffidence of my own merit I sometimes fear you will love me less after being so long from me — if you should may my life end before I know it that I may die thinking you wholy mine — Adieu my love L K

REVOLUTIONARY WAR LETTER FROM ALEXANDER HAMILTON, 1780: In this letter to a French diplomat, Alexander Hamilton, aide-de-camp to General Washington and future Secretary of the Treasury, cannot refute his correspondent's gloomy view of the American Revolution. By October 1780, Hamilton was discouraged with the lack of resources for the Continental Army and the ineffectuality of Congress. Such experiences during the war informed Hamilton's ideas about the need for a strong central government after the Revolution was won.

In my absence from Camp, the Commissary of prisoners has no doubt informed you, that your Brothers were not at New York. I am sorry you were so long kept in suspense about an explanation which without a determined disposition to blunder ought to have been long since obtained.

I find, my Dear Sir, on the experiment in several ways, that I cannot regularly procure the New York papers in exchange for those of Philadelphia. The only certain mode would be to send a weekly flag for the purpose, but the General apprehensive of popular jealousies, thinks it would be inconvenient. I shall with pleasure continue to forward them as often as they come into my hands; but I will not give you the trouble of sending regularly those of Philadelphia, as the object you have in view cannot be answered by it.

We are again told of an embarkation on the point of sailing three days since. We have been so often **deceived that we are diffident of accounts of this kind; but the present come with a degree of emphasis, that entitle them to attention. No particulars. The want of money makes us want every thing else even intelligence.**

I have received since my return several letters from you, I agree with you my Dear Sir that while we call to our friends for help, we ought to help ourselves; and I am mortified that we seem not to be in a disposition to do it, the late deliberations on our military affairs prove that we have not profitted by experience; still the same system of feebleness and temporary expedients. Misfortune may at last enlighten us, but it may come too late to do any thing more
^ **than to make our darkness visible and discover to us sights of woe. I confess I view our affairs in a gloomy light, We hear there is to be a Congress of the neutral powers to meet at the hague this winter to mediate a peace, God send it we want one.**

Permit me to repeat to you the assurances of my attachment.
A Hamilton

October 12th. 80

deceived that we are diffident of accounts of this kind; but the present come with a degree of emphasis, that intitle them to attention — No ^particulars! The want of money makes us want every thing else — even ~~all~~ intelligence.

I have received since my ~~last~~ return several letters from you — I agree with you my Dear Sir that while we call to our friends for help, we ought to help ourselves; and I am mortified that we seem not to be in a disposition to do it — The late deliberations on our military affairs prove that we have not profitted by experience; ~~still~~ the same system of feebleness and temporary expedients: Misfortune may at last ~~make~~ ~~us~~ enlighten us; but it may ~~come to late to do any thing more~~ than to make our "darkness visible" and discover to us sights of woe" — I confess I view our affairs in a gloomy light — We hear there is to be a Congress of the neutral powers to meet at the hague this winter to mediate a peace — God send it — we want one.

Permit me to repeat to you the assurances of my attachment

A Hamilton —

October 12.   80.

Page 2 of Alexander Hamilton's two-page letter to François, the Marquis de Barbé-Marbois, October 12, 1780. From the Gilder Lehrman Collection, GLC 12.

9

GEORGE WASHINGTON LETTER AGAINST SLAVERY, 1786: In this letter to a fellow Virginian and plantation owner, George Washington expresses his aversion to the institution of slavery: "I never mean . . . to possess another slave by purchase." He looks to the legislature to adopt a plan by which "slavery in this Country may be abolished by slow, sure, & imperceptable degrees."

Mount Vernon 9th Sep 1786

Dear Sir,

     Your favor of the 20th. ulto. did not reach me till about the first inst. It found me in a fever, from which I am now but sufficiently recovered to attend to business. I mention this to shew that I had it not in my power to give an answer to your propositions sooner.

     With respect to the first. I never mean (unless some particular circumstances should compel me to it) to possess another slave by purchase; it being among my first
the Legislature by
wishes to see some plan adopted by ⌃ which slavery in this Country may be abolished by slow, sure, & imperceptable degrees. With respect to the 2d., I never did, nor never intend to purchase a military certificate; I see no difference it makes with you (if it is one of the funds allotted for the discharge of my claim) who the the purchaser is. If the depreciation is 3 for 1 only, you will have it in your power whilst you are at the receipt of Custom - Richmond - where it is said the great regulator of this business (Greaves) resides, to convert them into specie at that rate. If the difference is more, there would be no propriety, if I inclined to deal in them at all, in my taking them at that exchange.

     I shall rely on your promise of Two hundred pounds in five Weeks from the date of your letter. It will enable me to pay the workmen which have been employed abt. this house all the Spring & Summer, (some of whom are here still). But there are two debts which press hard upon me. One of which, if there is no other resource, I must sell land or negroes to discharge. It is owing to Govr. Clinton of New York, who was so obliging as to borrow, & become my security for £ 2500 to answer some calls of mine. This sum was to be returned in twelve months from the conclusion of the Peace. For the remains of [struck: this sum], about Eight hundred pounds york Cy. I am now paying an interest of Seven pr. Ct., but the high interest (tho' more than any estate can bear) I should not regard, if my credit was not at stake to comply with the conditions of the loan. The other debt, tho' I know the person to whom it is due wants it, and I am equally anxious to pay it, might be put of [sic] a while longer. This sum is larger than the other.

I am. Dr Sir

Yr Most Obedt Hble Ser

Mount Vernon 9th Sept 1786

Dear Sir,

Your favor of the 20th ulto. did not reach me till about the first inst. — It found me in a fever, from which I am now but sufficiently recovered to attend to business. — I mention this to shew that I had it not in my power to give an answer to your propositions sooner, —

With respect to the first. I never mean (unless some particular circumstances should compel me to it) to possess another slave by purchase; it being among my first wishes to see some plan adopted by the legislature by which slavery in this country may be abolished by slow, sure, & imperceptable degrees. — With respect to the 2d, I never did, nor never intend to purchase a military certificate; — I see no difference it makes with you (if it is one of the funds allotted for the discharge of my claim) who the the purchaser is

is

Page 1 of a three-page letter from George Washington to John Mercer, September 9, 1786.
From the Gilder Lehrman Collection, GLC 3705.

WE the People of the States of New-Hampſhire, Maſſachuſetts, Rhode-Iſland and Providence Plantations, Connecticut, New-York, New-Jerſey, Pennſylvania, Delaware, Maryland, Virginia, North-Carolina, South-Carolina, and Georgia, do ordain, declare and eſtabliſh the following Conſtitution for the Government of Ourſelves and our Poſterity.

ARTICLE I.

The ſtile of this Government ſhall be, " The United States of America."

II.

The Government ſhall conſiſt of ſupreme legiſlative, executive and judicial powers.

III.

The legiſlative power ſhall be veſted in a Congreſs, to conſiſt of two ſeparate and diſtinct bodies of men, a Houſe of Repreſentatives, and a Senate ; ~~each of which ſhall, in all caſes, have a negative on the other.~~ The Legiſlature ſhall meet on the firſt Monday in December in every year. *unleſs a different day ſhall be appointed by Law –*

At leaſt Once every Year & such meeting ſhall be on the firſt monday &ca

IV.

Sect. 1. The Members of the Houſe of Repreſentatives ſhall be choſen every ſecond year, by the people of the ſeveral States comprehended within this Union. The qualifications of the electors ſhall be the ſame, from time to time, as thoſe of the electors in the ſeveral States, of the moſt numerous branch of their own legiſlatures.

Sect. 2. Every Member of the Houſe of Repreſentatives ſhall be of the age of ~~twenty-five years at leaſt ;~~ ſhall have been a citizen *of* the United States for at leaſt ~~three~~ *ſeven* years before his election ; and ſhall be, at the time of his election, a *inhabitant* ~~reſident~~ of the State in which he ſhall be choſen.

Sect. 3. The Houſe of Repreſentatives ſhall, at its firſt formation, and until the number of citizens and inhabitants ſhall be taken in the manner herein after deſcribed, conſiſt of ſixty-five Members, of whom three ſhall be choſen in New-Hampſhire, eight in Maſſachuſetts, one in Rhode-Iſland and Providence Plantations, five in Connecticut, ſix in New-York, four in New-Jerſey, eight in Pennſylvania, one in Delaware, ſix in Maryland, ten in Virginia, five in North-Carolina, five in South-Carolina, and three in Georgia.

Sect. 4. As the proportions of numbers in the different States will alter from time to time ; as ſome of the States may hereafter be divided ; as others may be enlarged by addition of territory ; as two or more States may be united ; as new States will be erected within the limits of the United States; the Legiſlature ſhall, in each of theſe caſes, regulate the number of repreſentatives by the number of inhabitants, according to the proviſions herein after made, ~~by the rate~~ of one for every forty thouſand. *Provided every State ſhall have* *not exceeding* *one Repreſentative*

hereafter mentioned the rule for direct Taxation Article 7 Section 3

Sect. 5. All bills for raiſing or appropriating money, and for fixing the ſalaries of the officers of government, ſhall originate in the Houſe of Repreſentatives, and ſhall not be altered or amended by the Senate. No money ſhall be drawn from the public Treaſury, but in purſuance of appropriations that ſhall originate in the Houſe of Repreſentatives. *This out*

Sect. 6. The Houſe of Repreſentatives ſhall have the ſole power of impeachment. It ſhall chooſe its Speaker and other officers.

Sect. 7. Vacancies in the Houſe of Repreſentatives ſhall be ſupplied by writs of election from the executive authority of the State, in the repreſentation from which they ſhall happen. *the ſame being notified by the Speaker of the Houſe*

V.

U.S. CONSTITUTION, FIRST DRAFT, 1787: *Printed as the basis for the delegates' deliberations at the Constitutional Convention in August 1787, this copy was owned by Pierce Butler, a delegate from South Carolina, whose handwritten notes and emendations are visible throughout. The preambles to the draft – "We the People of the States of . . ." – and to the final version – "We the People of the United States" – show that in the six weeks between the writing of the draft and of the final version the idea of a united nation had been born.* (Page 1 of the first draft of the U.S. Constitution, August 6, 1787. From the Gilder Lehrman Collection, GLC 819.01.)

For Jonathan Williams Esq
from B Franklin

WE, the People of the United States, in order to form a more perfect union, establish justice, insure domestic tranquility, provide for the common defence, promote the general welfare, and secure the blessings of liberty to ourselves and our posterity, do ordain and establish this Constitution for the United States of America.

ARTICLE I.

Sect. 1. ALL legislative powers herein granted shall be vested in a Congress of the United States, which shall consist of a Senate and [House] of Representatives.

Sect. 2. The House of Representatives shall be composed of members chosen every second year by the people of the several states, and the electors in each state shall have the qualifications requisite for electors of the most numerous branch of the state legislature.

No person shall be a representative who shall not have attained to the age of twenty-five years, and been seven years a citizen of the United States, and who shall not, when elected, be an inhabitant of that state in which he shall be chosen.

Representatives and direct taxes shall be apportioned among the several states which may be included within this Union, according to their respective numbers, which shall be determined by adding to the whole number of free persons, including those bound to service for a term of years, and excluding Indians not taxed, three-fifths of all other persons. The actual enumeration shall be made within three years after the first meeting of the Congress of the United States, and within every subsequent term of ten years, in such manner as they shall by law direct. The number of representatives shall not exceed one for every thirty thousand, but each state shall have at least one representative; and until such enumeration shall be made, the state of New-Hampshire shall be entitled to chuse three, Massachusetts eight, Rhode-Island and Providence Plantations one, Connecticut five, New-York six, New-Jersey four, Pennsylvania eight, Delaware one, Maryland six, Virginia ten, North-Carolina five, South-Carolina five, and Georgia three.

When vacancies happen in the representation from any state, the Executive authority thereof shall issue writs of election to fill such vacancies.

The House of Representatives shall chuse their Speaker and other officers; and shall have the sole power of impeachment.

Sect. 3. The Senate of the United States shall be composed of two senators from each state, chosen by the legislature thereof, for six years; and each senator shall have one vote.

Immediately after they shall be assembled in consequence of the first election, they shall be divided as equally as may be into three classes. The seats of the senators of the first class shall be vacated at the expiration of the second year, of the second class at the expiration of the fourth year, and of the third class at the expiration of the sixth year, so that one-third may be chosen every second year; and if vacancies happen by resignation, or otherwise, during the recess of the Legislature of any state, the Executive thereof may make temporary appointments until the next meeting of the Legislature, which shall then fill such vacancies.

No person shall be a senator who shall not have attained to the age of thirty years, and been nine years a citizen of the United States, and who shall not, when elected, be an inhabitant of that state for which he shall be chosen.

The Vice-President of the United States shall be President of the senate, but shall have no vote, unless they be equally divided.

The Senate shall chuse their other officers, and also a President pro tempore, in the absence of the Vice-President, or when he shall exercise the office of President of the United States.

The Senate shall have the sole power to try all impeachments. When sitting for that purpose, they shall be on oath or affirmation. When the President of the United States is tried, the Chief Justice shall preside: And no person shall be convicted without the concurrence of two-thirds of the members present.

Judgment in cases of impeachment shall not extend further than to removal from office, and disqualification to hold and enjoy any office of honor, trust or profit under the United States; but the party convicted shall nevertheless be liable and subject to indictment, trial, judgment and punishment, according to law.

Sect. 4. The times, places and manner of holding elections for senators and representatives, shall be prescribed in each state by the legislature thereof; but the Congress may at any time by law make or alter such regulations, except as to the places of chusing Senators.

The Congress shall assemble at least once in every year, and such meeting shall be on the first Monday in December, unless they shall by law appoint a different day.

Sect. 5. Each house shall be the judge of the elections, returns and qualifications of its own members, and a majority of each shall constitute a quorum to do business; but a smaller number may adjourn from day to day, and may be authorised to compel the attendance of absent members, in such manner, and under such penalties as each house may provide.

Each house may determine the rules of its proceedings, punish its members for disorderly behaviour, and, with the concurrence of two-thirds, expel a member.

Each house shall keep a journal of its proceedings, and from time to time publish the same, excepting such parts as may in their judgment require secrecy; and the yeas and nays of the members of either house on any question shall, at the desire of one-fifth of those present, be entered on the journal.

Neither house, during the session of Congress, shall, without the consent of the other, adjourn for more than three days, nor to any other place than that in which the two houses shall be sitting.

Sect. 6. The senators and representatives shall receive a compensation for their services, to be ascertained by law, and paid out of the treasury of the United States. They shall in all cases, except treason, felony and breach of the peace, be privileged from arrest during their attendance at

the

U.S. Constitution, final version, 1787: *The final text of the Constitution was printed on September 17, 1787 and distributed to the delegates, among whom Benjamin Franklin, aged eighty-one, was the senior member. Franklin signed this copy as a gift for his nephew Jonathan Williams.* (Page 1 of the final draft of the U.S. Constitution, inscribed by Benjamin Franklin to Jonathan Williams, printed by Dunlap & Claypoole on September 17, 1787. From the Gilder Lehrman Collection, GLC 3585.)

Hamilton-Burr duel, 1804: *Mere hours after the duel between Alexander Hamilton, former Secretary of the Treasury, and Vice President Aaron Burr in 1804, Angelica Church, Hamilton's sister-in-law, expresses her futile hope that he would recover. The hasty scrawl of her handwriting suggests the degree of her distress.*

---

at Wm. Bayards Greenwich
Wednesday Morn

My dear Brother

I have the painful task to inform you that General Hamilton was this morning woun[d]ed by that <u>wretch Burr</u> but we have every reason to hope that he will recover. May I advice that you repair immediately to my father, as perhaps he may wish to come down - My dear Sister bears with saintlike fortitude this affliction.

The Town is in consternation; and there exists only the <u>expression of Grief</u> & Indignation.

Adieu my dear Brother remember me to Sally, ever yours

A Church

At Mr. Bayards Greenwich
Wednesday Morn

My dear Brother

I have the painful task to inform you that General Hamilton was this morning wounded by that wretch Burr, but we have every reason to hope that he will recover. my dear sir I advise that you repair immediately to my father, as perhaps he may wish to come down — My dear Sister bear with saintlike fortitude this Affliction.

The Town is in consternation, and there exists only the expression of grief & Indignation.

Adieu my dear Brother remember me to Sally, ever yours A Church

Angelica Church's letter to her brother Philip J. Schuyler, July 11, 1804.
From the Gilder Lehrman Collection, GLC 7882.

AMISTAD SLAVE REBELLION, 1839: *This 19th-century ad for a book on the* Amistad *incident dramatizes the heroism of the Africans who revolted against their enslavement in 1839. The book promises a detailed account of how "the African captives . . . in order to obtain their freedom and return to Africa rose upon the Captain and the crew of the vessel."*

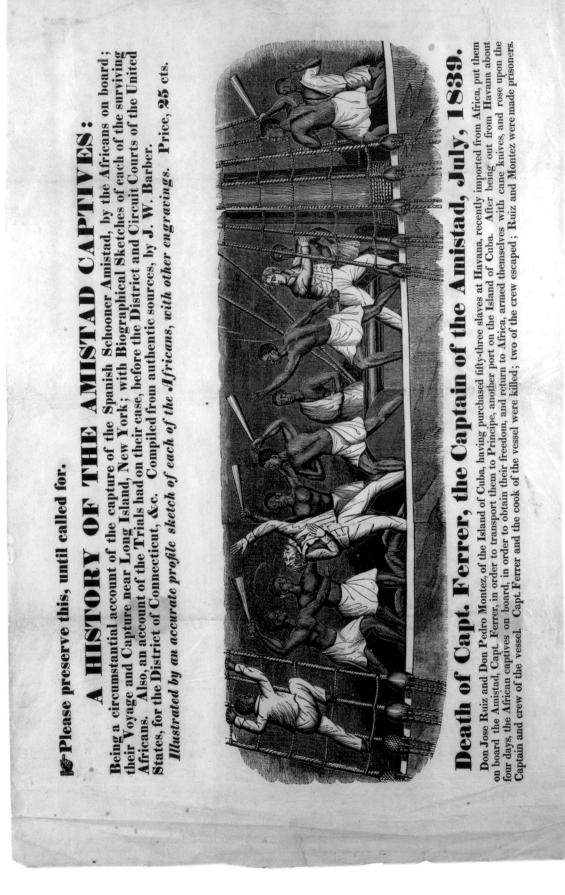

☞ Please preserve this, until called for.

A HISTORY OF THE AMISTAD CAPTIVES:

Being a circumstantial account of the capture of the Spanish Schooner Amistad, by the Africans on board; their Voyage and Capture near Long Island, New York; with Biographical Sketches of each of the surviving Africans. Also, an account of the Trials had on their case, before the District and Circuit Courts of the United States, for the District of Connecticut, &c. Compiled from authentic sources, by J. W. Barber. *Illustrated by an accurate profile sketch of each of the Africans, with other engravings.* Price, 25 cts.

Death of Capt. Ferrer, the Captain of the Amistad, July, 1839.

Don Jose Ruiz and Don Pedro Montez, of the Island of Cuba, having purchased fifty-three slaves at Havana, recently imported from Africa, put them on board the Amistad, Capt. Ferrer, in order to transport them to Principe, another port on the Island of Cuba. After being out from Havana about four days, the African captives on board, in order to obtain their freedom, and return to Africa, armed themselves with cane knives, and rose upon the Captain and crew of the vessel. Capt. Ferrer and the cook of the vessel were killed; two of the crew escaped; Ruiz and Montez were made prisoners.

"Death of Capt. Ferrer," an advertisement for John Warner Barber's *A History of the Amistad Captives*, New Haven, Conn., 1840. From the Gilder Lehrman Collection, GLC 4295.

JOHN QUINCY ADAMS AND THE AMISTAD CASE, 1840: *Abolitionists had written to John Quincy Adams asking him to represent the* Amistad *captives before the Supreme Court. Here, with characteristic humility, Adams accepts, hoping he will "do justice to their cause." Adams spoke before the Court for nine hours, which moved the majority to decide in favor of the captives.*

Roger S. Baldwin, Esqr. New Haven Conn[ecticu]t.

Boston 11. Novr. 1840.

Dear Sir

I have received your obliging Letters of the 2d. and 4th: instt together with the narrative of the case to be tried before the Supreme Court of the United States, at their next January Session, of the Captives of the Amistad.

I consented with extreme reluctance at the urgent request of Mr. Lewis Tappan and Mr. Ellis Gray Loring, to appear before the Court as one of the Counsel for these unfortunate men. My reluctance was founded entirely and exclusively upon the consciousness of my own incompetency to do justice to their cause. In every other point of view there is in my estimation no higher object upon earth of ambition than to occupy that position.

I expect to leave this city next Monday the 16th instt. for Hartford; and hope to be the next Morning Tuesday the 17th at New Haven. I shall then desire to see and converse with you concerning the case and will if necessary devote the day to that object. I have engaged to be at New York on the 18th.

I am with great respect Dear Sir

Your obedt Servt   J. Q. Adams

Roger S. Baldwin Esqr. New-Haven Connt.

Boston 11. Novr 1840.

Dear Sir

I have received your obliging Letters of the
2d. and 4th. instt together with the narrative of the case to be tried
before the Supreme Court of the United States, at their next January
Session, of the Captives of the Amistad.

I consented with extreme reluctance at the urgent
request of Mr Lewis Tappan and Mr Ellis Gray Loring, to appear
before the Court as one of the Counsel for these unfortunate men.
My reluctance was founded entirely and exclusively upon the
consciousness of my own incompetency to do justice to their cause
In every other point of view there is in my estimation no higher
object upon earth of ambition than to occupy that position.

I expect to leave this city next Monday, the 16th instt
for Hartford; and hope to be the next Morning Tuesday the 17th at
New-Haven – I shall then desire to see and converse with you
concerning the case, and will if necessary devote the day to that
object I have engaged to be at New-York on the 18th.

I am with great respect Dear Sir
Your obedt. Servt.   J. Q. Adams

FREDERICK DOUGLASS LETTER TO HIS FORMER OWNER, 1857: *Following his escape from slavery in Maryland to freedom in New York City in 1838, Frederick Douglass became a leader of the abolition movement and its best-known orator. Here, in an extraordinary display of forgiveness, Douglass writes to Hugh Auld, his former master: "I love you, but hate slavery."*

Rochester Oct. 4th 1857

Hugh Auld Esq.
          My dear sir:

                My heart tells me that you are too noble to treat with indifference the request I am about to make. It is twenty years since I ran away from you, or rather not from you but from <u>Slavery</u>, and since then I have often felt a strong desire to hold a little correspondence with you and to learn something of the position and prospects of your dear children. They were dear to me and are still indeed I feel nothing but kindness for you all. I love you, but hate slavery. Now my dear sir, will you favor me by dropping me a line, telling me in what year I came to live with you in Aliceanna St. the year the Frigate was built by Mr. Beacham. The information is not for publication - and shall not be published. We are all hastening where all distinctions are ended, kindness to the humblest will not be unrewarded. Perhaps you have heard that I have seen <u>Miss Amanda</u> that was, Mrs. Sears that is, and was treated kindly such is the fact. Gladly would I see you and Mrs. Auld or Miss Sopha as I used to call her. I could have lived with you during life in freedom though I ran away from you so unceremoniously. I did not know how soon I might be sold. But I hate to talk about that. A

line from you will find me Addressed Fred^k Douglass
Rochester N. York.   I am dear sir very truly yours,   Fred: Douglass

Rochester Oct. 4th (1857

Hugh Auld Esq

My dear Sir.

My heart tells me that
you are too noble to treat with indifference the
request I am about to make, It is twenty years
since I ranaway from you, or rather not from you
but from Slavery, and since then I have often felt
a strong desire to hold a little correspondence with you
and to learn something of the position and prospects
of your dear children— They were dear to me— and
are still— indeed I feel nothing but kindness for
you all— I love you, but hate Slavery, Now my
dear Sir, will you favor me by dropping me a line, telling
me in what year I came to live with you in Aliceanna st
the year the "Frigate was built by Mr. Beacham—
The information is not for publication— and shall
not be published— We are all hastening where all
distinctions are ended, kindness to the humblest will
not be unrewarded
Perhaps you have heard that I have seen Miss Amanda
that was, Mrs Sears that is, and was treated kindly
Such is the fact, Gladly would I see you and Mrs.
Auld— or Miss Sopha as I used to call her.
I could have lived with you during life in freedom
though I ranaway from you so unceremoniously,
I did not know how soon I might be sold. But I hate
to talk about that, A line from you will find me Addressed Fredk Douglass
Rochester N. York. I am dear sir very truly yours, Fred: Douglass

Hugh Auld's handwritten copy of Frederick Douglass's letter to Hugh Auld, October 4, 1857.
From the Gilder Lehrman Collection, GLC 7484.06.

ABRAHAM LINCOLN SPEECH NOTES, 1858: *In these speech notes, Abraham Lincoln offers an early formulation of the ideas he would advance in his campaign for the U.S. Senate in 1858. Lincoln identified slavery as a moral and political issue that threatened the continued existence of the United States. Invoking the biblical passage "A house divided against itself can not stand," he declared, "I believe this government can not endure permanently half slave and half free."*

———————————————————————

Why, Kansas is neither the <u>whole</u>, nor a <u>tithe</u> of the real question.

"A house divided against itself can not stand"

I believe this government can not endure permanently half slave, and half free.

I expressed this belief a year ago; and subsequent developments have but confirmed me.

I <u>do</u> not expect the Union to be dissolved. I do not expect the house to fall; but I do expect it will cease to be divided. It will become <u>all</u> one thing, or <u>all</u> the other. Either the opponents of slavery will arrest the further spread of it, and put it in course of ultimate extinction; or its advocates will push it forward till it shall become alike lawfull in <u>all</u> the states, old, as well as new. Do you doubt it? Study the Dred Scott decision, and then see, how little, even now, remains to be done.

That decision may be reduced to three points. The first is, that a negro can not be a citizen. That point is made in order to deprive the negro in every possible event, of the benefit of that provision of the U. S. Constitution which declares that: "The <u>citizens</u> of each State shall be entitled to all previleges and immunities of citizens in the several States."

The second point is, that the U. S. constitution protects slavery, as property, in all the U. S. territories, and that neither congress, nor the people of the territories, nor any other power, can prohibit it, at any time prior to the formation of State constitutions.

This point is made, in order that the territories may safely be filled up with slaves, <u>before</u> the formation of State constitutions, and thereby to embarrass the free state sentiment, and enhance the chances of slave constitutions being adopted.

The third point decided is that the voluntary bringing of Dred Scott into Illinois by his master, and holding him here a long time as a slave, did not operate his emancipation, did not make him free.

Why, Kansas is neither the whole, nor a tithe of the real question—

"A house divided against itself can not stand."

I believe this government can not endure, permanently, half slave, and half free—

I expressed this belief a year ago; and subsequent developements have but confirmed me.

I do not expect the Union to be dissolved— I do not expect the house to fall; but I do expect it will cease to be divided— It will become all one thing, or all the other. Either the opponents of slavery will arrest the further spread of it, and put it in course of ultimate extinction; or its advocates will push it forward till it shall become alike lawful in all the states, old, as well as new— Do you doubt it? Study the Dred Scott decision, and then see, how little, even now, remains to be done—

That decision may be reduced to three points— The first is, that a negro can not be a citizen— That point is made in order to deprive the negro, in every possible event, of the benefit of that provision of the U. S constitution which declares that; "The citizens of each State shall be entitled to all privileges and immunities of citizens in the several States."

The second point is, that the U. S constitution protects slavery, as property, in all the U. S. territories, and that neither congress, nor the people of the territories, nor any other power, can prohibit it, at any time prior to the formation of State constitutions—

This point is made, in order that the territories may safely be filled up with slaves, before the formation of State constitutions, and thereby to embarrass the free state

A fragment of Abraham Lincoln's "House Divided" speech, 1857-1858.
From the Gilder Lehrman Collection, GLC 2533.

ABRAHAM LINCOLN, 1860 AND 1863: *Appearing confident and youthful at age fifty-one, Lincoln would come to show on his physiognomy the suffering of the next few years.*
(Photographs of Abraham Lincoln, by Alexander Hesler, June 3, 1860 and Alexander Gardner, November 1863. From the Gilder Lehrman Collection, GLC 4200 and GLC 245.)

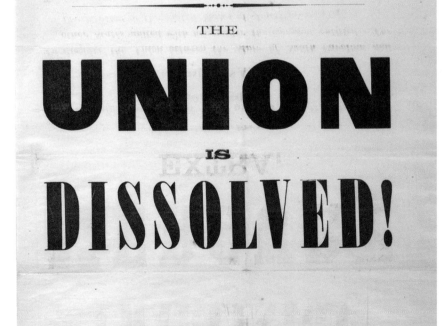

South Carolina Secession, December 1860: *The November 1860 election of Abraham Lincoln convinced Southern states that the federal government would initiate judicial and legal action against slavery. This broadside was printed in Charleston, South Carolina, on December 20, 1860, when South Carolina voted to repeal the Constitution of the United States and seceded from the Union. The Constitution of the new Confederacy would sanction the unrestricted right to hold slaves.* ("The Union is Dissolved," December 20, 1860. From the Gilder Lehrman Collection, GLC 2688.)

WIFE OF UNION SOLDIER DESCRIBES WAR HOSPITAL, 1862: *James Kelly served with the 14th Indiana Volunteers beginning in 1861. In March 1862 his wife Mary traveled to the field hospital in Winchester, Virginia, where he lay wounded, and wrote this letter home describing the terrible conditions in the hospital. Despite her efforts, James Kelly died of his wounds on May 8, 1862.*

Winchester
Monday 31 [1862]
Dear Sarah

    I arrived here last night (Sunday) by hard traveling though we missed the train near ? and was delayed about a day. Found Mr. Kelly very sadly wounded indeed. His recovery very doubtful though some such cases have been known to recover. He dont seem to suffer as much as I would expect under the circumstances. I hope Sis and mother are doing very well. You must stay with them. I hope I shall soon be able to come home. This is a bad place for a sick person. Perhaps I may try to take him on a train tomorrow in the direction of home. If I can get him taken so he won't have to be changed on the cars. There are some Pennsylvania wounded going tomorrow by the way of Philidelphia. It may be that I may go with them. He dont think he will ever get over it and is prepared to go. Seems perfectly resigned. He dont complain much. I think my fate is right hard. **trouble every spring. The wounded are dying every day. This is a three story building and very large at that and every room is full. its very sad times indeed.**

    I will write again in a few days. Perhaps I may send a dispatch if necessary.

    Tell Sis to be a good girl.

Mr. Kelly is wounded in the lower part of the abdomen injuring his bowels in some way a very serious wound indeed. I still hope he may be one of the exceptions in this case. If we remain here there wont be any Dr left thats any account for all the surgeons expect every day to be ordered on to their regiments about 20 miles from here. So if we can go we had better. Mr Slocum is going tomorrow he has his thigh broken but seems in good spirits. I think he will soon get well. The ladies here have been very kind to our men though there are plenty of Secesh here of the meanest kind.

    I would like to know how you are getting on. I hope Sis didnt get sick again.

Yours Truly Mary Kelly

trouble every spring The wounded are
dying every day This is a three story building and very large at that and every room
is full its very sad times indeed

I will write again in a few days
perhaps I may send a dispatch if necessary
Tell Sis to be a good girl

Mr Kelly is wounded in the lower part of the
abdomen injuring his bowels in some way
a very serious wound indeed I still hope
he may be one of the exceptions in this case
If we remain here there wont be any Sr left
thats any account for all the surgeons expect
every day to be ordered on to their regiments
about 20 miles from here So if we can go
we had better Mr Slocum is going tomorrow
he has his thigh broken but seems in
good spirits I think he will soon get
well the ladies here have been very kind
to our men though there are plenty of
secesh here of the meanest kind

I would like to know how you are
getting on I hope sis didnt get sick
again   Yours Truly Mary Kelly

Page 2 of Mary Kelly's two-page letter to her sister Sarah Gordon, ca. March 31, 1862.
From the Gilder Lehrman Collection, GLC 4197.25.

27

UNION SOLDIER WRITES ABOUT THE EMANCIPATION PROCLAMATION, 1862: John Jones was a Union soldier in Co. F, 45th Illinois Infantry. In this letter he responds enthusiastically to news reports that President Lincoln would issue an emancipation proclamation: "The year of Jubilee' has indeed come to the poor Slave. . . . The name of Abraham Lincoln will be handed down to posterity as one of the greatest benefactors of his country."

Jackson Tenn, Oct, 3/1862

My Dear Wife

I received your letter yesterday, and now proceed to answer it, as I have a little time on my hands this evening, and I do not know that I can spend it in a more profitable way. Certainly, I can not spend it in a more agreeable way than in writing to one in whom my fondest hopes of happiness are centered. It is just a year ago today Mary that I became a servant of Uncle Sam. I hardly thought then that I should have to be a soldier so long as a year, but now I don't know but my chance is good for a year or two more. Well one third of my time is served at any rate, even if the war lasts so long, but I do not think it will. **It must close by next spring, if it does not I shall almost begin to think that we never ought to whip them. Thank God a new era has dawned, the car of liberty ᴀ civilisation is rolling on. I**

have reference to the Presidents proclamation. The "Year of Jubilee" has indeed come to the poor slave. The proclamation is a deathblow to slavery, because without doubt a majority of the slaves states will be in arms against the Government on the 1st of January 1862 [sic]. The name of Abraham Lincoln will be handed down to posterity, as one of the greatest benefactors of his country, not surpassed by the immortal Washington himself. It is what I have expected, and what I have hoped for. We now know what we are fighting for, we have, an object, and that object is avowed. Now we may expect that the armies of the Union will be victorious, that an Omnipotent and just God will favor us, and crown our efforts with success. Oh! what a day for rejoicing will it be, when America the boasted "land of the free and home of the brave" shall have erased from its fair escutcheon the black stain of human slavery. The majority of the people, and the soldiers will sustain the President in his act, it is well received by the army in this department, believed to be the right thing at the right time.

It must close by next Spring, if it does not I shall almost begin to think that we never ought to whip them. Thank God a new era has dawned, the car of liberty, and civilisation is rolling on. I have reference to the Presidents proclamation, The "Year of Galilee" has indeed come to the poor Slave The proclamation is a deathblow to Slavery, because without doubt a majority of the Slave States will be in Arms against the Government on the 1st of January 1862 The name of Abraham Lincoln will be handed down to posterity, as one of the greatest benefactors of his Country. not surpassed by the immortal Washington himself. It is what I have expected, and what I have hoped for, We now know what we are fighting for, we have an object, and that object is avowed Now we may expect that the armies of the Union will be victorious, that an Omnipotent and just God will favor us, and crown our efforts with Success. Oh! what

Page 2 of John Jones' eight-page letter to his wife, October 3, 1862.
From the Gilder Lehrman Collection, GLC 5981.09.

29

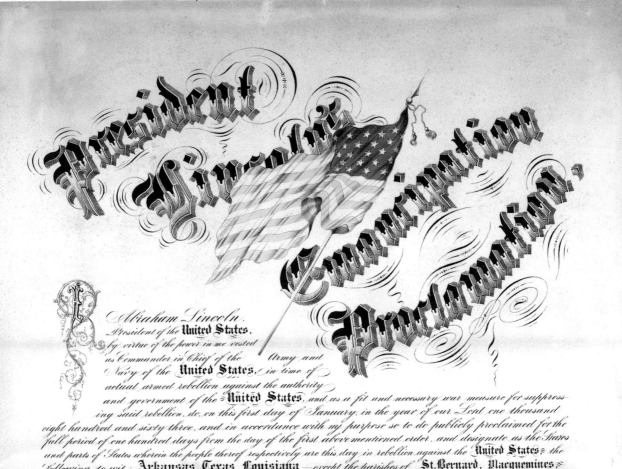

THE EMANCIPATION PROCLAMATION, 1864: *Issued January 1, 1863, it was a carefully crafted document in which Lincoln, as commander in chief, justified emancipation as a military act against the states in rebellion. This unique copy of a rare lithograph, designed by a fourteen-year-old boy in California, was sent to Washington, D.C., where Lincoln signed it.* ("Emancipation Proclamation," engraving published in San Francisco, 1864, signed by Abraham Lincoln. From the Gilder Lehrman Collection, GLC 742.)

MEN OF COLOR
TO ARMS! TO ARMS!
NOW OR NEVER

This is our golden moment! The Government of the United States calls for every Able-bodied Colored Man to enter the Army for the

Three Years' Service!

And join in Fighting the Battles of Liberty and the Union. A new era is open to us. For generations we have suffered under the horrors of slavery, outrage and wrong; our manhood has been denied, our citizenship blotted out, our souls seared and burned, our spirits cowed and crushed, and the hopes of the future of our race involved in doubt and darkness. But now our relations to the white race are changed. Now, therefore, is our most precious moment. Let us rush to arms!

FAIL NOW, & OUR RACE IS DOOMED

On this the soil of our birth. We must now awake, arise, or be forever fallen. If we value liberty, if we wish to be free in this land, if we love our country, if we love our families, our children, our home, we must strike now while the country calls; we must rise up in the dignity of our manhood, and show by our own right arms that we are worthy to be freemen. Our enemies have made the country believe that we are craven cowards, without soul, without manhood, without the spirit of soldiers. Shall we die with this stigma resting upon our graves! Shall we leave this inheritance of Shame to our Children! No! a thousand times NO! We WILL Rise! The alternative is upon us. Let us rather die freemen than live to be slaves. What is life without liberty! We say that we have manhood; now is the time to prove it. A nation or a people that cannot fight may be pitied, but cannot be respected. If we would be regarded men, if we would forever silence the tongue of Calumny, of Prejudice and Hate, let us Rise Now and Fly to Arms! We have seen what Valor and Heroism our Brothers displayed at Port Hudson and Milliken's Bend, though they are just from the galling, poisoning grasp of Slavery, they have startled the World by the most exalted heroism. If they have proved themselves heroes, cannot WE PROVE OURSELVES MEN!

ARE FREEMEN LESS BRAVE THAN SLAVES

More than a Million White Men have left Comfortable Homes and joined the Armies of the Union to save their Country. Cannot we leave ours, and swell the Hosts of the Union, to save our liberties, vindicate our manhood, and deserve well of our Country. MEN OF COLOR! the Englishman, the Irishman, the Frenchman, the German, the American, have been called to assert their claim to freedom and a manly character, by an appeal to the sword. The day that has seen an enslaved race in arms has, in all history, seen their last trial. We now see that our last opportunity has come. If we are not lower in the scale of humanity than Englishmen, Irishmen, White Americans and other Races, we can show it now. Men of Color, Brothers and Fathers, we appeal to you, by all your concern for yourselves and your liberties, by all your regard for God and humanity, by all your desire for Citizenship and Equality before the law, by all your love for the Country, to stop at no subterfuge, listen to nothing that shall deter you from rallying for the Army. Come Forward, and at once Enroll your Names for the Three Years' Service. Strike now, and you are henceforth and forever Freemen!

E. D. Bassett,	Rev. J. Underdue,	P. J. Armstrong,	Rev. J. C. Gibbs,	Elijah J. Davis,
William D. Forten,	John W. Price,	J. W. Simpson,	Daniel George,	John P. Burr,
Frederick Douglass,	Augustus Dorsey,	Rev. J. B. Trusty,	Robert M. Adger,	Robert Jones,
Wm. Whipper,	Rev. Stephen Smith,	S. Morgan Smith,	Henry M. Cropper,	O. V. Catto,
D. D. Turner,	N. W. Depee,	William E. Gipson,	Rev. J. B. Reeve,	Thos. J. Dorsey,
Jas. McCrummell,	Dr. J. H. Wilson,	Rev. J. Boulden,	Rev. J. A. Williams,	I. D. Cliff,
A. S. Cassey,	J. W. Cassey,	Rev. J. Asher,	Rev. A. L. Stanford,	Jacob C. White,
A. M. Green,	James Needham,	Rev. Elisha Weaver,	Thomas J. Bowers,	Morris Hall,
J. W. Page,	Ebenezer Black,	David B. Bowser,	J. C. White, Jr.,	J. P. Johnson,
L. R. Seymour,	James R. Gordon,	Henry Minton,	Rev. J. P. Campbell,	Franklin Turner,
Rev. William T. Catto,	Samuel Stewart,	Daniel Colley.	Rev. W. J. Alston,	Jesse E. Glasgow.

A Meeting in furtherance of the above named object will be held

And will be Addressed by

U. S. Steam-Power Book and Job Printing Establishment, Ledger Buildings, Third and Chestnut Streets, Philadelphia.

BLACK SOLDIERS JOIN UNION ARMY, 1863: *Following the Emancipation Proclamation, Frederick Douglass and other abolitionists joined in a national call for black men to enlist in the Union army. This recruiting poster printed in Philadelphia in 1863 makes a powerful appeal in the name of various leaders in the African-American community. By the war's end more than 200,000 African Americans had served in the Union military forces.* ("Men of Color, to Arms! to Arms!" recruitment broadside, published in Philadelphia, Pa., 1863. From the Gilder Lehrman Collection, GLC 2752.)

BLACK SOLDIER'S CIVIL WAR DIARY, 1864: *These pages describing the bravery of black troops in the siege of Petersburg, Virginia, appear in the manuscript diary of William P. Woodlin, an African-American soldier in the Union army. Woodlin's diary, which spans December 1863 to October 1864, is still unpublished and is believed to be the only surviving diary of an African-American Civil War soldier.*

28th   We had guard mount as usual this morning & then Rec'd marching orders at 3 P.M. When the whole Corps were moved down towards the pontoon Bridge with the supposition that we were going to Bermuda Hundred, we crossed at Broad way landing but went to Deep Bottom where we arrived between one & two A.M., lay down until 4 when we made coffee & **left our knapsacks & got under way, when we soon got under fire in the same old place, but they were driven-out by the 18th Corps & the first line of trenches were carried; we continued to advance untill 3 PM when we came to the 4th line on the New Market road where our brigade made a charge one at a time but they were repulsed. our Regt leaving 65 men in all the 7th lost three whole Cos. captured. We held our position that night but the Johnnies made a furious attack on the 30th three times but were repulsed with great loss; by the colored troops of the 10th & 18th Corps which there formed a junction. there was a tremendous fire of shells, grape & canister and the like loss about 10 wounded in our Regt. things quiet with the exception of the sharpshooters.**
Oct 1st   **Very rainy, but a heavy attack expected it was delayed for some reason or other. though the [Rear] continued to shell our lines, a piece coming clear to the Hospital a goodly No of prisoners were taken on Friday of the 8th Carolina.**
2nd   **The Regt was engaged in fatigue work all day no firing near us heavy on the extreme left & a little on the right a few prisoners taken.**
Oct 3rd   **Still engaged in fatigue, tore an old house down last night I got some of the boards this morning & a little mail.**
4th   **went to the rear to wash** & clean up.

& left our knapsacks & got under way, when we soon got under fire in the same old place, but they were driven out by the 18th Corps & the first line of entrenches were carried; we continued to advance untill 3 PM when we came to the 4th line on the New Market road where our brigade made a charge one at a time but they were repulsed, our Regt loosing 65 men in all the 7th lost three whole Co's captured. We held our position that night but the Johnnies made a furious attack on the 30th three times but were repulsed with great loss; by the colored troops of the 10th & 18th Corps which there formed a junction there was a tremendous fire of shells grape & canister and the like

loss about 10 wounded in our Regt. things quiet with the exception of the sharpshooters.

Oct 1st Very rainy, but a heavy attack expected it was delayed for some reason or other. though the Rebs continued to shell our lines, a piece coming clear to the Hospital a goodly No of prisoners were taken on Friday of the 8th Carolina & 2d The Regt was engaged in fatigue work all day no firing near us heavy on the extreme left & a little on the right a few prisoners taken

Oct 3 Still engaged in fatigue, tore an old house down last night I got some of the boards this morning & a little mail.
4th went to the rear to wash

United States Military Telegraph,

War Department.

76

Washington, June 15, 1864

Lieut. Gen. Grant

Head Qrs. A. P.

Have just read your despatch of 1 P.m. yesterday. I begin to see it. You will succeed. God bless you all.

A. Lincoln

56
84

LINCOLN TELEGRAM TO GENERAL GRANT, 1864: *Despite his frustrations with previous commanders and continuing heavy casualties under General Ulysses S. Grant, Lincoln came to see that Grant's overall strategy was the right one to win the war. In this telegram written in the early hours of the morning after a typical long night vetting incoming reports, Lincoln for the first time expresses his confidence in Grant's strategic vision.* (Abraham Lincoln's handwritten telegram to Ulysses S. Grant, June 15, 1864. From the Gilder Lehrman Collection, GLC 1572.)

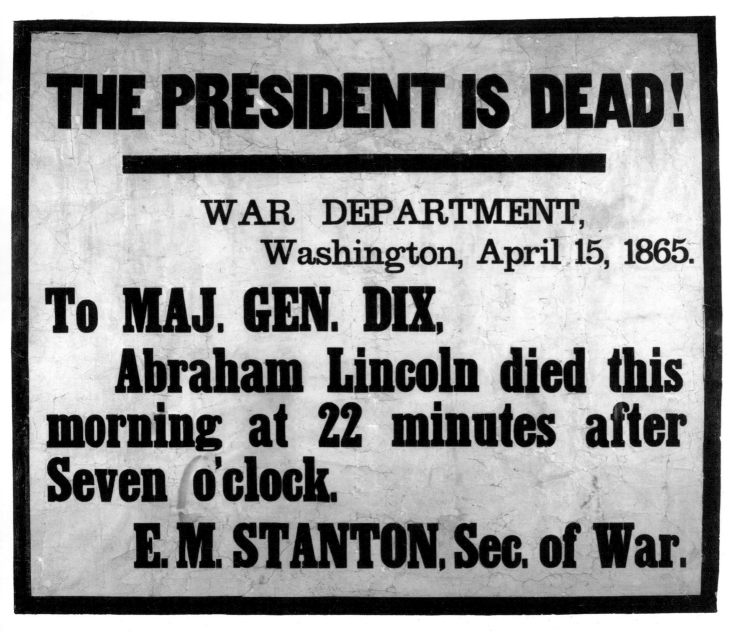

THE PRESIDENT IS DEAD, 1865: *Lincoln's assassination sent shockwaves through the nation. This poster, printed in New York City, was spread throughout the streets to inform the public about the national disaster.* ("The President Is Dead!" printed in New York, April 1865. From the Gilder Lehrman Collection, GLC 6680.)

FREDERICK DOUGLASS LETTER TO MARY TODD LINCOLN, 1865: *Over the course of the Civil War, and despite initial differences, Frederick Douglass and President Lincoln forged a relationship based on a shared vision. After Lincoln's assassination, Mrs. Lincoln presented Douglass with the President's favorite walking stick as a memento, and in this letter Douglass poignantly expresses his thanks.*

Rochester N.Y. August 17, 1865.

Mrs. Abraham Lincoln:

Dear Madam: Allow me to thank you, as I certainly do thank you most sincerely for your thoughtful kindness in making me the owner of a cane which was formerly the property and the favorite walking staff of your late lamented husband the honored and venerated President of the United States.

I assure you, that this inestimable memento of his Excellency will be retained in my possession while I live — an object of sacred interest — a token not merely of the kind consideration in which I have reason to know that President was pleased to hold me personally, but as an indication of his humane interest [in the] welfare of my whole race.

With every proper sentiment of Respect and Esteem
I am, Dear Madam, your Obedt Servt.
Frederick Douglass.

Rochester. N.Y. August 17. 1865.

Mrs Abraham Lincoln:

Dear Madam: Allow me to thank you, as I certainly do thank you most sincerely for your thoughtful kindness in making me the owner of a Cane — which was formerly the property and the favorite walking Staff of your late lamented husband, the honored and venerated President of the United States.

I assure you, that this inestimable memento of his Excellency will be retained in my possession while I live — an object of sacred interest — a token not merely of the kind consideration in which I have reason to know that the President was pleased to hold me personally, but as an indication of his humane ~~consideration~~ interest [in the] welfare of my whole race.

With every proper sentiment of Respect and Esteem

I am, Dear Madam, your Obedt Servt

Frederick Douglass.

Frederick Douglass's letter to Mary Todd Lincoln, August 17, 1865.
From the Gilder Lehrman Collection, GLC 2474.

POSTWAR AMENDMENTS BRING CIVIL RIGHTS TO AFRICAN AMERICANS, 1870: *The passage of the Thirteenth, Fourteenth and Fifteenth Amendments gave constitutional status to emancipation's promise of freedom. The artist depicts African Americans' hopes for their future under freedom: the right to education, a stable family life, jobs, and the vote. Surrounding the scene of celebration in Washington, D.C., are portraits of Frederick Douglass, John Brown, and Abraham Lincoln.* From the Gilder Lehrman Collection, GLC 2917.

SUSAN B. ANTHONY MEMORANDUM ABOUT WOMEN'S RIGHTS, 1901: *Writing at the age of eighty, having just retired from a long public life as an advocate for abolitionism and women's rights, Susan B. Anthony trenchantly summarizes the gains that have been made in women's rights. Her energetic tone suggests the inner resilience that had carried her so far and would propel the movement far into the 20th century.*

The one purpose of my life has been the establishment of perfect Equality of rights for women – civil and political – industrial and educational. We have attained equal chances in nearly all of the colleges and universities – equal chances to work – but not equal pay. We have school suffrage in half the states, taxpayers' suffrage in a half-dozen states – Municipal suffrage in one state – Kansas – and full suffrage in four – Wyoming, Colorado, Utah, Idaho – and hope and work in faith till the end.

    In good cheer

        Susan B. Anthony

Nov. 7.1901 –   Rochester, N.Y.

The one purpose of my life has been the establishment of perfect Equality of rights for women — civil and political — industrial and educational — We have attained equal chances in nearly all of the colleges & universities — equal chances to work — but not equal pay — we have school suffrage in half the states, Taxpayers' suffrage in a half-dozen states — Municipal suffrage in one state — Kansas — and full suffrage in four — Wyoming, Colorado, Utah, Idaho — and hope and work in faith till the end —

In good cheer

Susan B. Anthony

Rochester, N.Y.

Nov. 7. 1901 —

Manuscript on her work for equal rights for women by Susan B. Anthony, November 7, 1901.
From the Gilder Lehrman Collection, GLC 7337.

ADVICE SHEET

D. W. GRIFFITH'S

"THE BIRTH OF A NATION"

The following information is for House Managers, and should be carefully observed:

Play date _____

Company arrives _____ from _____ via _____ Ry.

Company leaves _____ for _____

Manager with company is _____

Musical Director is _____

Chief Operator is _____

We carry Musical Director, Violin, Cornet, Drums.

_____

It is very important that your projection machines are well oiled and thoroughly cleaned, in order that best results be attained.

It is vitally important that you have PIANO in tune (International Pitch) and three music stands with lights attached for our musicians, as well as shaded lamp atop piano.

Have all cuts, slides, photographs and clippings of newspaper advertisements ready for our manager on his arrival.

Please bear in mind that NEGROES MUST NOT BE ADMITTED TO "THE BIRTH OF A NATION" under any circumstance.

If by any chance you have any paper left over please deliver it to company manager. Paper costs money and can be used in other towns.

Where possible it is advisable to have reserved seats for the night performance, at least. Tickets should be placed on sale some days in advance of play date, and the public acquainted with the fact that reserved seat tickets are procurable.

Yours very truly,

JACK EDWARDS,
Southern Representative.

Permanent address
Box 1294
Atlanta, Ga.

THE BIRTH OF A NATION, 1915: *This is a rare surviving copy of the "Advice Sheet" that was distributed with D. W. Griffith's film* The Birth of a Nation *to theaters when the film was released in 1915. Significantly, the distributors are adamant that "NEGROES MUST NOT BE ADMITTED . . . under any circumstance." The deeply racist film nonetheless attracted a wide audience, but also stirred controversy and protests from the newly created NAACP.* (Blank advice sheet for *The Birth of a Nation*, 1915. From the Gilder Lehrman Collection, GLC 5091.)

May 30, 1934

FOR THE PRESS

323

CONFIDENTIAL UNTIL RELEASED

CAUTION: This address of the President at Gettysburg, Pennsylvania, today, May 30, 1934, MUST BE HELD FOR RELEASE and no portion, synopsis or intimation is to be published or given out until its delivery has actually begun.
CAUTION: Care must be exercised to avoid premature publication.

STEPHEN EARLY
Assistant Secretary to the President

GETTYSBURG ADDRESS

My Friends:

On these hills of Gettysburg two brave armies of Americans once met in combat. Not far from here, in a valley likewise consecrated to American valor, a ragged Continental Army survived a bitter winter to keep alive the expiring hope of a new Nation; and near to this battle-field and that valley stands that invincible city where the Declaration of Independence was born and the Constitution of the United States was written by the fathers. Surely, all this is holy ground.

It was in Philadelphia, too, that Washington spoke his solemn, tender, wise words of farewell -- a farewell not alone to his generation, but to the generation of those who laid down their lives here and to our generation and to the America of tomorrow. Perhaps if our fathers and grandfathers had truly heeded those words we should have had no family quarrel, no battle of Gettysburg, no Appomattox.

As a Virginian, President Washington had a natural pride in Virginia; but as an American, in his stately phrase, "the name of American, which belongs to you, in your National capacity, must always exalt the just pride of Patriotism, more than any appellation derived from local discrimination."

Recognizing the strength of local and State and sectional pre-judices and how strong they might grow to be, and how they might take from the National Government some of the loyalty the citizens owed to it, he made three historic tours during his Presidency. One was through New England in 1789, another through the Northern States in 1790, and still another through the Southern States in 1791. He did this, as he said, "In order to become better acquainted with their principal characters and internal circumstances, as well as to be more accessible to numbers of well informed persons who might give him useful advices on political subjects."

But he did more to stimulate patriotism than merely to travel and mingle with the people. He knew that Nations grow as their commerce and manufactures and agriculture grow, and that all of these grow as the means of transportation are extended. He sought to knit the sections to-gether by their common interest in these great enterprises; and he pro-jected highways and canals as aids not to sectional, but to national development.

But the Nation expanded geographically after the death of Washington far more rapidly than the Nation's means of inter-communication. The small national area of 1789 grew to the great expanse of the Nation of 1860. Even in terms of the crude transportation of that day, the thirteen states were but within "driving distance" of each other.

With the settling and the peopling of the Continent to the shores of the Pacific, there developed the problem of self-contained territories because the Nation's expansion exceeded its development of means of transportation. The early building of railroads did not pro-ceed on national lines.

FRANKLIN D. ROOSEVELT SPEAKS AT GETTYSBURG, 1934: Invited to speak at Gettysburg in 1934, President Franklin D. Roosevelt shrewdly avoided any comparison with Lincoln's famous speech by immediately shifting his focus to the heroism of George Washington and his troops at Valley Forge, "not far from here." Roosevelt proceeds to enlist Washington as a proponent of canals, highways and other national infrastructure to place FDR's own national program of public works in the favorable light of illustrious historic precedent. (Franklin D. Roosevelt's press release of a speech delivered at Gettysburg, Pa., in 1934. From the Gilder Lehrman Collection, GLC 3352.)

Pres

THE WHITE HOUSE
WASHINGTON

January 14, 1942

Mr. Joseph Curran, President
National Maritime Union
346 West 17th Street
New York, N. Y.

My dear Mr. Curran:

I am informed that the discrimination against colored seamen, referred to in your telegram of January 2nd, was eliminated by the action of the United States Maritime Commission on the day it occurred.

It is the policy of the Government of the United States to encourage full participation in the National Defense program by all citizens, regardless of race, creed, color, or national origin, in the firm belief that the democratic way of life within the nation can be defended successfully only with the help and support of all groups within its borders.

The policy was stated in my Executive Order signed on June 25, 1941. The order instructed all parties making contracts with the Government of the United States to include in all defense contracts thereafter a provision obligating the contractor not to discriminate against any worker because of race, creed, color or national origin.

Questions of race, creed and color have no place in determining who are to man our ships. The sole qualifications for a worker in the maritime industry, as well as in any other industry, should be his loyalty and his professional or technical ability and training.

Sincerely yours,

Franklin D. Roosevelt

LETTER FROM PRESIDENT FRANKLIN D. ROOSEVELT FORBIDDING DISCRIMINATION, 1942: *The mobilization of men and women for the war effort inevitably brought racial issues to the fore. In this letter, FDR signals his disapproval of discrimination against blacks in all branches of the service, including the merchant marine.* (Franklin D. Roosevelt's executive order on racial discrimination, 1942. From the Gilder Lehrman Collection, GLC 6686.)

which were built with federal Hill-Burton Act financial assistance. The Department asked the court to declare unconstitutional the separate-but-equal provision of the act. While the Department was permitted to intervene, the court subsequently dismissed the suit, filed by Negro doctors, dentists and patients. An appeal appears likely.

Employment Suit: Problems of racial discrimination are by no means peculiar to the South. The Department appeared as a friend of the court in an appeal to the Colorado Supreme Court by a Negro pilot who charged he was denied employment with an airline in violation of a state anti-discrimination law. The Colorado court denied the appeal, but the Supreme Court of the United States has agreed to review the case.

Police Brutality: During 1962, the Department brought 15 police brutality prosecutions, many of them in Northern states. These cases included one in Indiana where two Negro detectives were convicted of brutally beating a Negro defendant to coerce him to confess several crimes.

In summary, 1962 was a year of progress for the United States in the field of civil rights. This is not to say the problems are disappearing. They remain, and they remain difficult -- not only in the South, with open discrimination, but throughout the country where Negroes are the victims of school "resegregation", bias in housing, or employment, or other facets of society. Ugly incidents like the Mississippi riot may occur again.

But we are accelerating our progress. Again, let me say this acceleration occurs in large measure because of the emerging spirit of the South. In 1962 this spirit was not the brutal one of rioting and violence at the University of Mississippi. The spirit was that exemplified in Georgia last week by Governor Carl E. Sanders, in his inaugural address.

"We revere the past," he said. "We adhere to the values of respectability and responsibility which constitute our tradition." Then he added, "We believe in law and order and in the principle that all laws apply equally to all citizens."

Sincerely,

Attorney General

The President,
The White House,
Washington, D. C.

ATTORNEY GENERAL ROBERT KENNEDY ON CIVIL RIGHTS IN 1962: *At the end of 1962, President Kennedy asked his brother, Attorney General Robert Kennedy, to compile a report on the Civil Rights enforcement activities of the Justice Department over the previous year. In this, the final sheet of a nine-page report, Robert Kennedy notes "progress" overall, but reminds the President that difficult race problems remain "not only in the South . . . but throughout the country."* (Robert Kennedy's Report to the President on civil rights, 1962. From the Gilder Lehrman Collection, GLC 5630.)

ABOLITIONIST CAMPAIGN TOKEN, 1838: *Beginning with Josiah Wedgwood in England in the 1780s, abolitionists had distributed images of enslaved Africans under the motto "Am I Not a Man and a Brother" as part of their anti-slavery campaigns. This token, which was issued in the United States in 1838, incorporated the motto as part of the escalating abolitionist movement in the decades leading up to the Civil War.* (Anti-slavery token, 1838. From the Gilder Lehrman Collection, GLC 8551.)

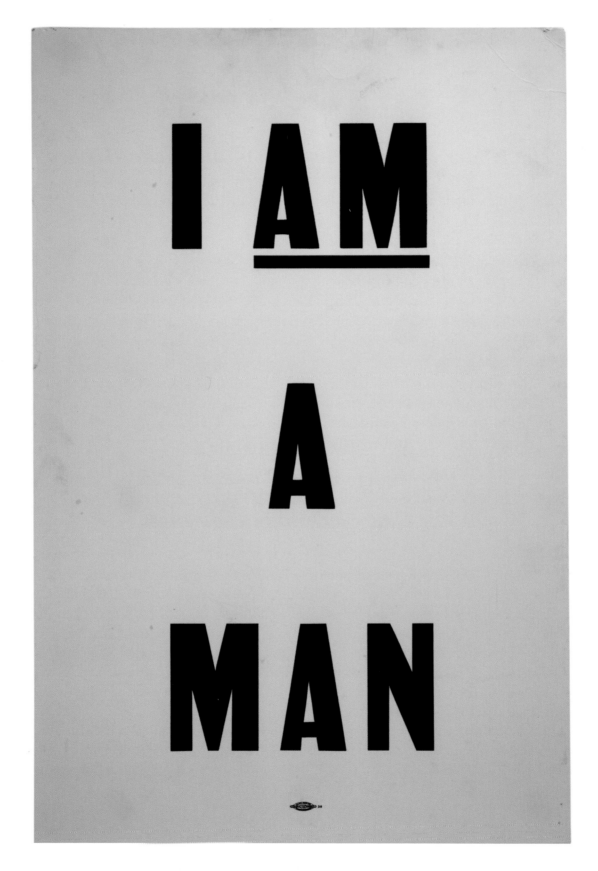

MARTIN LUTHER KING, JR. AND CIVIL RIGHTS, 1968: *On April 4, 1968, the day he was assassinated, Martin Luther King, Jr. traveled to Memphis to lead a peaceful march of garbage workers striking for equitable wages. The marchers carried these placards inscribed "I AM A MAN," echoing the famous anti-slavery slogan, "Am I Not a Man and a Brother." ("I AM A MAN" civil rights poster, April 4, 1968. From the Gilder Lehrman Collection, GLC 6124.)*

The Gilder Lehrman Institute of American History

The Gilder Lehrman Institute of American History promotes the study and love of American history through:

- Public lectures, conferences, and exhibitions
- Research fellowships for scholars in American history
- Summer seminars and enrichment programs for school teachers
- Books, essays, journals, and curriculum guides on American history
- Electronic resources for students, teachers, scholars, and the general public
- History high schools and Saturday academies in New York and school districts across the country
- Annual prizes for the best books on Lincoln and the Civil War, slavery and abolition, and other fields

To learn more about the Gilder Lehrman Institute of American History, please visit

www.gilderlehrman.org

The Gilder Lehrman Collection

The Gilder Lehrman Collection, on deposit at the New-York Historical Society in New York City, includes more than 60,000 American historical documents. Its manuscripts, books, prints, broadsides, photographs and other artifacts range from the era of Columbus to modern times. Most of the materials focus on European colonization, the American Revolution, the Constitution, early nationalism and sectionalism, the ante-bellum period, and the Civil War. Richard Gilder and Lewis Lehrman formed the collection to "collect, preserve and study the historical record" of the United States, particularly to save privately owned manuscripts and make them available to scholars and educators.

For more information, please visit www.gilderlehrman.org or contact the Curator for the Collection, Sandra Trenholm, at the Gilder Lehrman Collection, New-York Historical Society, 170 Central Park West, New York, NY 10024, or by e-mail at reference@gilderlehrman.com.